Take a Stand Against Bullying

CYBER BULLYING

Rachel Stuckey

Crabtree Publishing Company

Author: Rachel Stuckey

Publishing plan research and development:
Sean Charlebois, Reagan Miller
Crabtree Publishing Company

Project coordinator: Kathy Middleton

Editorial director: Melissa McClellan

Art director: Tibor Choleva

Fictional Introductions: Rachel Stuckey

Editors: Kristine Thornley, Molly Aloian

Proofreader: Kelly McNiven

Production coordinator: Margaret Amy Salter

Prepress technician: Margaret Amy Salter

Print coordinator: Katherine Berti

Developed and produced by: BlueApple Works Inc.

Consultant:
Adina Herbert, MSW, RSW
Social Worker, Youth Addictions and Concurrent Disorders Service
Centre for Addiction and Mental Health, Toronto, ON, Canada

Photographs: Front cover: Thinkstock; Title page, p.8: © Sylvie Bouchard/ Shutterstock Inc.; Contents page: © Ilike/ Shutterstock Inc.; p.4 © Christine Langer-Pueschel/ Shutterstock Inc.; p.6 © Vietrov Dmytro/ Shutterstock Inc.; p.7 © Peter Close/ Shutterstock Inc.; p.9, 29, 36 © Monkey Business Images/ Shutterstock Inc.; p.10 © Eduardo Cervantes/ Shutterstock Inc.; p.11 © DmitriMaruta/ Shutterstock Inc.; p.12, 30 © Lisa F.Young/ Shutterstock Inc.; p.13 © RimDream/ Shutterstock Inc.; p.14 © Elena Elisseeva/ Shutterstock Inc.; p.15 © SergiyN/ Shutterstock Inc.; p.16 © Dragon Images/ Shutterstock Inc.; p.17 © rangizzz/ Shutterstock Inc.; p.18 © Tootles/ Shutterstock Inc.; p.20 © enciktat/ Shutterstock Inc.; p.21 © flydragon/ Shutterstock Inc.; p.22 © dgmata/ Shutterstock Inc.; p.23 © mirana/ Shutterstock Inc.; p.24 © Jess Yu /Shutterstock Inc.; p.25 © Jaimie Duplass/ Shutterstock Inc.; p.26 © Redav /Shutterstock Inc.; p.27 © Petrenko Andriy/ Shutterstock Inc.; p.28 © Pablo Calvog/ Shutterstock Inc.; p.31 © Sanjay Deva/ Shutterstock Inc.; p.32 © Chris Curtis/ Shutterstock Inc.; p.33 © Masson/ Shutterstock Inc.; p.34 © Natalin★ka/ Shutterstock Inc.; p.35 © leungchopan/ Shutterstock Inc.; p.37 © Sascha Burkard/ Shutterstock Inc.; p.38 © Eric Fahrner/ Shutterstock Inc.; p.39 © George Muresan/ Shutterstock Inc.; p.40 © rmnoa357/ Shutterstock Inc.; p.43 © Paulius Brazauskas; torn paper background © LeksusTuss; banners: © Amgun/ Shutterstock Inc.

Library and Archives Canada Cataloguing in Publication

Stuckey, Rachel
    Cyber bullying / Rachel Stuckey.

(Take a stand against bullying)
Includes index.
Issued also in electronic format.
ISBN 978-0-7787-7913-1 (bound).--ISBN 978-0-7787-7918-6 (pbk.)

    1. Cyberbullying--Juvenile literature. I. Title. II. Series: Take a stand against bullying

HV6773.15.C92S78 2013   j302.34'302854678   C2013-900254-5

Library of Congress Cataloging-in-Publication Data

Stuckey, Rachel.
    Cyber bullying / Rachel Stuckey.
       pages cm. -- (Take a stand against bullying)
    Includes index.
    ISBN 978-0-7787-7913-1 (reinforced library binding) -- ISBN 978-0-7787-7918-6 (pbk.) -- ISBN 978-1-4271-9074-1 (electronic pdf) -- ISBN 978-1-4271-9128-1 (electronic html)
    1. Cyberbullying--Juvenile literature. 2. Bullying--Prevention--Juvenile literature. 3. Internet and children--Juvenile literature. I. Title.

HV6773.15.C92S78 2013
302.34'302854678--dc23
                                        2013000584

Crabtree Publishing Company

www.crabtreebooks.com   1-800-387-7650

Printed in Canada/022013/BF20130114

Published in Canada
Crabtree Publishing
616 Welland Ave.
St. Catharines, ON
L2M 5V6

Published in the United States
Crabtree Publishing
PMB 59051
350 Fifth Avenue, 59th Floor
New York, NY 10118

Published in the United Kingdom
Crabtree Publishing
Maritime House
Basin Road North, Hove
BN41 1WR

Published in Australia
Crabtree Publishing
3 Charles Street
Coburg North
VIC, 3058

CONTENTS

Kayla felt the phone in her pocket buzz. She had another message, but she was afraid to look. Last week, she and her best friend, Marta, got into a fight about Marta's boyfriend—Kayla admitted that she had a crush on him, too. They hadn't spoken since, but Kayla had been getting **anonymous** messages on her phone.

The messages were pretty mean. Some just said "slut" and others said she was "ugly" and "stupid." She was pretty sure Marta was sending them, but the messages came from different **instant message** accounts so she wasn't absolutely sure. She had already sent Marta a message telling her to leave her alone. But, most of the girls in her class seemed to be siding with Marta, so Kayla decided to eat lunch by herself.

After lunch, when Kayla was in the computer lab, she opened an email from an account she didn't recognize. There was a picture attached—Kayla's head had been added to a picture of a naked woman with the word SLUT written across the picture. Kayla deleted the email right away.

On her way home from school, a boy from another class told her that she had an awesome body, and then laughed and walked away. Somehow, the photo sent to her had been sent to this boy too. She realized that probably everyone in the school had seen that photo by now.

Kayla didn't know what to do. She was humiliated and felt sick to her stomach. She told her parents she didn't feel well and wasn't hungry for dinner, and then she went to her room and cried.

The next day, Kayla was supposed to sing in the school's talent show. But she couldn't bear the idea of the whole school watching her and thinking of that fake picture. In the morning, she told her parents she was sick—she really did feel sick—and she stayed home from school. Kayla spent the day in bed dreading the idea of having to go back to school—ever.

The Nature of Cyber Bullying

Kayla is the victim of **cyber bullying**, a type of **bullying** that uses electronic devices and the Internet. Cyber bullying is a lot like social bullying, i.e., bullying to embarrass or humiliate another and often happens at the same time.

The results of cyber bullying are emotional and social, but cyber bullying can also have **traumatic** consequences. In 2012, a teenager named Amanda Todd from British Columbia, Canada, killed herself after suffering from cyber bullying for several years. After being stalked by an online predator, Amanda was targeted by her peers both online and at school. Amanda's case was very extreme, but many of the things that happened to her could happen to anyone in any community.

In this book, you will learn about different types of cyber bullying. You will learn how to avoid being a cyber bully and what to do if you are a **target** of a cyber bully. You'll also learn how cyber bullying hurts us all, and the long-term consequences of bullying in the digital world.

TAKE A STAND AGAINST
STOP
BULLYING

"Being bullied over the Internet is horrible. In person, maybe a few people will hear the insults. Over the Internet, the whole school can. It's torment and it hurts. Insults really hurt and sometimes it takes forever to heal."
Rebecca, age 13

CHAPTER 1
What is Cyber Bullying?

Cyber bullying includes sending or posting hurtful, embarrassing, or threatening text or images on the Internet, or through cell phones or other digital communication devices. Cyber bullying is intended to harm someone's social reputation, humiliate them, or scare them. Cyber bullies can reach a wide group of people very quickly. Cyber bullying often occurs behind the target's back. Once they are posted on the Internet, pictures and text never disappear so cyber bullying often leads to other kinds of bullying. As a result, cyber bullying may be the most dangerous type of bullying young people experience.

For many young people, cyber bullying can be social death. Cyber bullying can be very public, but the bullies often remain anonymous. Cyber bullying is often treated like entertainment by the bystanders— those people who read the websites and text messages, but are not directly involved.

Traditional bullying is still more common than cyber bullying, but research shows that about one in four young people have engaged in some kind of online or digital **harassment**. The most common form of online harassment is calling people hurtful names, followed by pretending to be someone else, and spreading rumors.

Both Direct and Indirect

Direct bullying, such as physical attacks and verbal abuse, takes place in person. **Indirect bullying**, such as social bullying, involves spreading rumors and gossiping behind someone's back, or excluding someone from a social group. However, cyber bullying can also be direct. For example, a bully may send mean or threatening text messages directly to a target over the phone or via email. Indirect cyber bullying includes sending messages about targets to other people, posting comments on websites, or even creating fake **social media** profiles.

Types of Cyber Bullying

Cyber bullying includes many acts of verbal and **social bullying**, such as gossiping, spreading rumors, saying hurtful things, or sharing private information. But cyber bullying has a digital twist and can include any of the following:

- Sending or posting hurtful messages by email, cell phone, or social media
- Posting or sending untrue or private information
- Posting or sending embarrassing information or photographs to other people
- Getting other people to post or send hurtful messages
- Encouraging others to exclude someone from an online group
- Impersonating someone online
- Using another person's password to access their profile or email
- Creating websites designed to humiliate and embarrass someone

"My friends and I were bored one night so we made up a website that made fun of this kid in our school. We thought it was really funny and that no one would find out that we did it."
Carlos, age 17

"I wouldn't have said those things to someone's face. I wished I could take back the comments I made when I saw how hurt the girls we rated were. But you can't undo what you post online. I feel terrible.." Jayden, age 17

What Makes It Bullying?

Many friends and family members tease each other when they are young. In fact, playful teasing and joking is one way to establish a place in a social group. But it is important for everyone to know the difference between playful joking and bullying. So what's the difference between teasing and joking and bullying?

- Bullying is deliberate. A bully's intention is to hurt someone.

- Bullying is repeated. A bully often targets the same person again and again.

- Bullying is about power. A bully usually chooses targets who are vulnerable, and bullying those targets makes a bully feel more powerful.

Bullies and Their Targets

Cyber bullying has challenged our understanding of the bully. Bullies used to be the tough boys or mean girls who picked on weak kids on the playground. But cyber bullies can be shy and quiet—they find their power behind their computer screens. The majority of kids who cyber bully never bully in person.

? Did You Know?

You are more likely to become a cyber bully if you have been the target of online harassment. Boys and girls are equally likely to be the target of cyber bullying.

The targets of cyber bullying can be anyone. Some targets of cyber bullying are bullied in person, too. But the nature of cyber bullying means that anyone can be harassed online for any reason.

The **bystander** is a **witness** to the abuse, but is not involved.

Sometimes bystanders do something to stop the bully, but most of the time bystanders simply watch what is happening and stay quiet to protect themselves. When it comes to cyber bullying, bystanders take a more active role. When bystanders forward embarrassing messages or photos, they are actually becoming bullies themselves.

Twisted Entertainment

According to a 2008 cyber bullying survey from the University of Toronto, young people are most likely to encounter cyber bullying through instant messaging, followed by email, then websites for games and social networking. Today, more and more young people have cell phones, and also smartphones with cameras, video chat, and Internet access. This means that young people can be involved in cyber bullying 24 hours a day.

Cyber Bullying Affects Everyone

Reading a nasty blog post about someone in your school is different than watching a fellow student being physically or verbally abused right in front of you. You don't see the target's pain, so cyber bullying is easier to ignore. Most of us like to read celebrity gossip magazines and blogs, and for bystanders of cyber bullying, the gossip, rumors, and embarrassing pictures can be just like those in the celebrity gossip magazines and blogs. It's even more interesting because it involves people the bystanders know. Often, targets of cyber bullying suffer in silence, so bystanders don't see or even think about how painful a photo or website really is.

Bullies Also Hurt Themselves

Each time a bully hurts someone else, they're also hurting themselves. We all have a natural feeling of **empathy** toward other people—we don't like to see people suffer. Bullies often attack others when they are feeling insecure or unsure about themselves. Whenever bullies attack, they become even more emotionally removed from the suffering of their target. They learn to justify their actions and often convince themselves that their targets deserve to be bullied. Therefore, bullies often fail to develop the social skills needed to make and keep friends, like sharing, reciprocating, empathizing, and negotiating. This makes their own insecurity worse.

Because we do not see the direct effects of cyber bullying like we do with physical bullying, people have a higher likelihood of becoming a cyber bully.

! Think About It!

When does gossiping with your friends over instant message (IM) or text message or on social media websites become cyber bullying? What do you do when you read mean things about classmates online?

"One of my friends started hassling me by sending me nasty text messages and this carried on at school. I found this really upset me, I had trouble concentrating on school and started to feel really bad about myself. I told my parents, my friends, and a teacher. She was spoken to and the messages have now stopped. I also blocked her online." Nicole, age 12

CHAPTER 2
Messages That Hurt

One way that cyber bullies attack their targets is by sending hurtful, embarrassing, or threatening messages either directly to them or about them to others. There are many different ways to send these messages.

Cell Phones and Texting

More and more young people now have their own cell phones. Although many schools have restricted the use of phones in the classroom, students still use their phones throughout the day to communicate with their friends. Practically every cell phone has a built-in digital camera, making it easy to take photos and videos at any time in any place.

Young people often send personal messages and photographs to their friends or boyfriends and girlfriends. But even these can end up being embarrassing, either by accident or if the relationship ends and private photos are made public.

"It's one thing when you get made fun of at school, but to be bullied in your own home via your computer is a disgusting thing for someone to do. It makes me wonder how people can be so rude and disrespectful of others and it makes me lose faith in the human race. It decreases my self-esteem and I often wonder what I did to make someone treat me that way." James, age 15

Spreading Gossip

Smartphones complicate the issue even further because images and videos can be sent via email or text and posted to a website immediately, before the sender has a moment to think about the consequences. New smartphone apps are being created every day that can be misused by bullies—secret cameras, insult apps, apps that rate appearance, apps that list the user's dislikes—the list goes on and on.

Cell phones have also turbo-charged the rate that gossip spreads. Gossip is the casual sharing of information about people and events that's a natural activity in social groups. But **malicious gossip** is the spreading of nasty rumors and lies about someone. Malicious gossip can destroy a person's reputation and status in their peer group. Targets of malicious gossip often don't know who started the rumor or who knows about it. But when it's spread over text message, an entire school might know within a few minutes.

Instant Messages and Emails

Like text messaging, **instant messages** (IM) and emails are also used to cyber bully. Instant messaging can be done on many different devices, including computers, cell phones, and tablets, making it a popular means of communication. It's also possible to create anonymous emails and IM handles, allowing cyber bullies to attack their targets with less risk of being found out.

Did You Know?

Young people are usually at home when they get harassing messages. In the digital world, bullies have the power to enter our safe place.

Text Wars

Cell phones are used by over 80 percent of teens regularly, making them the most likely channel for cyber bullying. A text war or text attack is when a group of teens gang up on a target, sending hundreds, even thousands of text messages to their phone. The result is that the target goes way over their monthly text plan and then gets a huge phone bill!

Think About It!

How many texts do you send in a day? Do you use text messaging to gossip with your friends? How would you feel if you took an embarrassing photo of yourself and it became public? What would you do if your parents saw the photo?

"I found out that someone posted a question about me on Formspring. A girl I liked sent me a link to it. All the answers were really nasty and hateful I felt so bad. I wanted to hide and never go back to school. Just because you don't have to sign your name to a comment doesn't mean you should be so mean." Joshua, age 13

CHAPTER 3
Social Media and the Web

Sending messages is one way cyber bullies can attack their targets, either directly or indirectly, but social media provides a **forum** for indirect public bullying. Blogs, Facebook, Twitter, and other similar sites are places where rumors can be easily spread or hurtful messages can be posted to many readers instantaneously. In extreme cases, bullies have created fake profiles in their target's names.

When cyber bullies use blogs, websites, or social media, anonymity is common—we often don't know the real identities of the bloggers we follow. It's also very easy to set up a website at little or no cost. There's very little to stop cyber bullies from using a website or blog to attack their targets.

The nature of the World Wide Web means that this information and these websites can be read all over the world and never go away—not completely. Websites are archived, and copied, and you never know who has read or seen something and kept a copy for themselves.

The Danger of the Digital

Sometimes cyber bullying can begin accidentally—instant messages, texts, emails, tweets, and Facebook comments can be misunderstood and private messages can be sent unintentionally to the wrong people. Feelings can easily be hurt, and revenge is one reason given by young people for why they engage in cyber bullying behavior.

This is why everyone must be careful about what digital messages they send and what they do with messages once they receive them. Never respond to an email, message, or post in anger—take a breather, or you may regret what you send!

Did You Know?

Girls are just as likely to engage in cyber bullying behavior as boys.

Photos, Photos, Everywhere

On social networking sites, you can tag images with the names of people who are in the photo. Without strong privacy settings, tagged photos can be found when you search a person's name using an Internet search engine. Embarrassing photos can be added to anyone's profile this way. Once a photo is on the Internet, it never goes away. Even if the person who posted the photo deletes it, copies of that image will remain. It only takes a few seconds to make a mistake that is permanent.

Facebook's Community Standards

Facebook has a policy of community standards for its users. Bullying and harassment are included in this policy. Many specific acts of bullying are prohibited under other categories in the policy, such as violence and threats, **hate speech**, nudity and **pornography**, and identity and privacy. But Facebook can only deal with abusive behavior when it is reported. When you see something on Facebook that you think violates the website's community standards, show an adult you trust and then report it to Facebook right away.

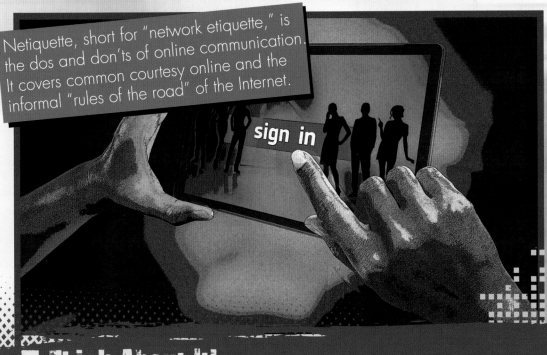

Netiquette, short for "network etiquette," is the dos and don'ts of online communication. It covers common courtesy online and the informal "rules of the road" of the Internet.

! Think About It!

What would you do if you told a friend something private and the next day you saw it on an anonymous blog about the people at your school? Do you follow any anonymous Twitter feeds about your school or community? When does an embarrassing photo of someone on Facebook go from a joke to harassment?

"I became a bully after I was bullied. I did it to get revenge on the girl who had posted mean comments about me in the chat room. I thought it would make me feel much better but I ended up feeling worse." Ashley, age 12

CHAPTER 4
Online Gaming

Multiplayer online games and virtual worlds are places where cyber bullying also occurs. When kids are playing or using the chat features to talk to other players, it is just like other types of digital communication and social networking.

It's normal in the heat of competition to "trash talk" your opponent, and it's even more common when you're playing games that are based on sports or combat and violence. It's easy, from the safety of your living room, to make statements that are more threatening or more nasty than you would make in person because there's little threat of retaliation outside the game world. But these kinds of comments can get out of hand, especially if they are made repeatedly toward the same opponent or go beyond the normal scope of the game.

Online Target

Taunting, pestering, insulting remarks and gestures, and nasty jokes are some of the ways that cyber bullies can abuse their targets in online games and virtual worlds. Even more than social media and text messages, online gamers are completely anonymous—it could be a player halfway around the world or it could be your next-door neighbor who is harassing you. Not knowing can make it seem even more threatening.

"I still cry when I think of what she emailed to me. After a while you start believing all of the things people tell you that aren't true. When I look in the mirror I wonder if I'm fat (I'm not)." Jessica, age 14

? Did You Know?

The virtual world has taken social bullying to the next level, and the lack of feedback or consequences can allow social conflict to quickly develop into bullying.

Rating Sites and Online Polls

One of the first forms of cyber bullying were rating websites like HOT or NOT or Rate My Face. Rating websites, or even review websites, are places where inappropriate comments and harassment can occur.

Similar to rating websites are online polls. There are many free survey and polling websites that let users create a simple poll and send it to a group of people via email. Young people can create polls about their peers, asking others to select the ugliest girl or the dumbest boy or the weirdest person in their school. These may seem like a joke, but they can be embarrassing and hurtful to others.

Aggressive Players

According to a 2008 report from the Pew Research Center's Internet & American Life Project, more than half of teens who play online video games report seeing or hearing people "being mean and overly aggressive" while playing and a quarter of them report that this happens "often."

Think About It!

Do you think "trash talk" is a normal part of an online game? How so? Have you ever been insulted or threatened or seen someone else be abused in an online game or virtual world? What did you do about it? Have you ever participated in a negative online poll about your classmates? Why?

"The Internet is not a place to harass others or hurt them. The Internet is supposed to be a place that is safe and fun for people, not a place to be criticized or harassed. Why not post something nice about someone instead of being mean. If you wouldn't say something to their face, don't say it about them online." Brianna, age 15

CHAPTER 5
Who's Involved?

Media reports on cyber bullying can make it seem like all teenagers are either victims of cyber bullies or they are cyber bullies themselves. That's simply not the case. However, like other forms of bullying, cyber bullying can get out of hand quickly. Although there are no physical scars, the effects of cyber bullying are damaging for everyone involved.

Understanding the Victim

Anyone can be the target of cyber bullying—even someone who is very popular in school and has a lot of friends. Cyber bullies can have a huge impact on their targets. If the bully is anonymous, targets don't know who to respond to or how to stop it. Cyber bullying has an unlimited number of witnesses, which can make it even more humiliating.

In addition to pain and embarrassment, cyber bullying also makes targets feel helpless. According to Be Web Aware (www.bewebaware.ca), over half of teenagers who are targets of cyber bullying never actually report it. Targets often don't know who is aware of the bullying, and when it's anonymous, targets don't know who they can trust. How do you report an attack that has no physical signs and is committed by a nameless and faceless attacker?

It is harder to get away from cyber bullies, because they can reach into your home from as far away as the other side of the world.

Understanding the Bully

It's much easier to hurt someone when you don't have to look them in the eye. We are all more likely to engage in cyber bullying than we are in traditional bullying. Cyber bullies can be shy, quiet, and nice in public. According to www.bewebaware.ca, one-quarter of youth who cyber bully are teenagers who have also bullied their peers offline. The rest do not bully others in person, which tells us that the digital world has created a new type of bully. Those who would never consider bullying in the physical world are doing so in the virtual world.

Technology has the power to change our **ethical behavior** because it doesn't provide the same feedback that in-person interaction does. We don't see the consequences of our actions or the social response. This lack of feedback can minimize our feelings of empathy or remorse.

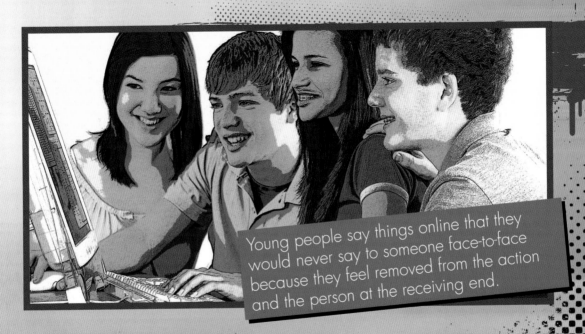

Young people say things online that they would never say to someone face-to-face because they feel removed from the action and the person at the receiving end.

The Role of the Bystander

A bystander is a person who witnesses an action or event but is not involved. When a fight breaks out in school, those who form the circle around the fighters are bystanders. Cyber bullying takes place in the virtual world, so the number of bystanders is almost limitless. Like the bully, bystanders may not see the effect cyber bullying has on its victims.

Unlike a fight in the cafeteria or in the schoolyard, cyber bullying usually happens away from adults. Therefore, bystanders have a very important role to play in stopping cyber bullying.

One study found that only half of young people who witnessed cyber bullying would rise up against the bully; the other half would simply go along with it.

Don't Just Stand By

Bystanders have the power to end—and even prevent—cyber bullying. Your first act as a helpful bystander is to refuse to pass on hurtful messages or photos, and to stop visiting blogs that are abusive. As a bystander, you can tell the bully to stop or that you are not interested in the gossip or mean comments. You can also publicly condemn bullies' actions on their blogs or Facebook pages—telling other bystanders that you don't think it's acceptable. You can even report what you witness to an adult. Most importantly, you can provide support to the target.

? Did You Know?

There is now an app for computers, smartphones, and tablets called Back Off Bully (BOB). The app lets you report an incident and asks you questions, gives you feedback, and sends the information to researchers for study.

"I think most people who bully online just do it to act tough, but since they're not saying it to someone's face it makes them seem like more of a wimp. I always try to step up for the bullied person." Paige, age 14

From Bystander to Bully

Bystanders who choose to ignore what they see are passively helping to continue the abuse through their own inaction. When bystanders pass on the gossip, nasty messages, or embarrassing photos, they are becoming bullies themselves. Encouraging a bully's behavior is just as bad as being the bully. A bystander who participates suffers the same negative consequences. They could get into trouble once the action is reported, and their feelings of empathy and remorse are affected also.

"I got this email that said really nasty things about a girl in my class. I forwarded it on to all my friends. Now I feel really bad, as bad as if I had written it myself."
Kim, age 13

? Did You Know?

According to a study done by Wired Safety (www.wiredsafety.org), 90 percent of middle-school students say they have been the victims of some sort of cyber bullying.

Why Don't More Bystanders Intervene?

It's very common for bystanders to keep quiet, even when they see someone in trouble—it's called the **bystander effect**. Research tells us that the more witnesses there are to an event, the lower the chances are that one of them will intervene. Researchers have been studying the bystander effect since the 1960s. Some witnesses are afraid to get involved, and when there are a lot of witnesses, most assume that someone else will deal with it. What we know for sure is that people who are educated about the bystander effect are far more likely to break free of it when they witness something wrong. Now that you know about it, don't be afraid to get involved.

Take action when you witness bullying. Don't assume that someone else will stand up against it—you have the power to help and you should use it.

Think About It!

How would you feel if you received a text message or email that made you uncomfortable, either about you or about another person? What would you do if you saw something mean about a friend posted on Facebook or another social media site? Have you spread rumors or posted embarrassing photos of your friends online? Why?

"I noticed that a lot of girls in my class were posting cruel comments on this other girl's Facebook page. I was scared that they would turn on me if I said something, so I talked to her and together we told the teacher about it. She told me she was really glad I spoke to her and that she didn't feel so hated." Noah, age 13

CHAPTER 6
Reporting Cyber Bullying

You have the power to stop cyber bullying. It may be that a group of your friends doesn't realize how dangerous it is to gossip online. They may not realize how much they are hurting someone when they share embarrassing photos or send mean text messages. Just asking your friends to stop and think about what they are doing can make a difference.

As a bystander, you can also refuse to participate in online gossip, you can defend the target of bullying, and you can offer the target of bullying your support so that he or she has a friend to confide in. You can also report incidents of cyber bullying to a responsible adult.

What to Do?

If you are being cyber bullied, you may experience many different emotions: anger, hurt, embarrassment, and fear. These emotions may lead you to seek revenge or try to avoid your friends or hide the experience from your family. It's important to remember that you are not powerless. There are things you can do to protect yourself and make it stop.

1. Don't respond. Don't retaliate.

2. Tell a trusted adult in your life.

3. Save all the evidence:
   - Do not delete or change any communications.
   - Save chats, emails, photos, text messages, etc.
   - Save copies or screen captures of websites and social media pages.
   - Print out whatever you can.

4. Block the harasser whenever possible.

5. Report the abuse using online reporting systems, if possible.

6. With the help of an adult, contact law enforcement.

Criminal Consequences

Naked and sexually suggestive pictures of people under the age of 18 are considered child pornography. It is illegal to take such pictures and share them with others or even have them in your possession. People who are found guilty of making, having, or sharing child pornography are considered sex offenders for the rest of their lives.

Other forms of cyber bullying may also be a criminal offense; there are laws against **hate crimes**, and harassment, revealing the identity of crime victims, and some communities have actual laws against bullying.

"I was online in a chat room and this guy was sexually harassing me by saying stuff to me and he wouldn't leave me alone. I had to exit the chat room and change my email."
Grace, age 14

It's OK to Tell!

When you were a little kid, you probably didn't like tattletales. Even today, you protect your friends instead of ratting them out. But there's a big difference between tattling or ratting out a friend and reporting dangerous behavior. When you tell an adult about bullying, you're not doing it to get someone in trouble, you're doing it to make the bully stop and to protect yourself, your peers, and even the bully. Whether you're the target or a bystander, you may not feel safe or comfortable confronting a bully yourself. It's important to report a bully's actions to someone who can protect the target. Some people may think you're a "rat" or a "snitch," but remember that reporting abuse of any kind is a courageous thing to do and everyone will be better off in the end.

Who to Tell

A trusted adult is someone you believe will listen and who has the ability and authority to help you. A trusted adult may be a parent or guardian, a teacher, or a counselor. Telling someone who fits that description what is happening isn't tattling. Sometimes all it takes is for a bully to be identified; but sometimes it takes more direct action, such as seeking help from the police. Even if the bullying only occurs at home, your school may also have rules against it.

? Did You Know?

Many victims of cyber bullying don't report the abuse because they are afraid they will lose their phones or access to the Internet. It's important for parents and guardians to keep an open mind and assure young people to tell them about bullying without the fear of losing their online privileges.

! Think About It!

If you saw a bigger kid push one of your classmates to the ground and steal her phone, would you go to help her and then report what you saw? What would you do if that same kid posted on Facebook that your classmate was stupid, or a freak, or a loser? Which kind of bullying do you think hurts more? What do you think about the old rhyme "sticks and stones may break my bones but words will never hurt me"?

CHAPTER 7
Beating the Bullies

Sometimes there's nothing you can do to stop a bully until after they hurt someone. There will always be a bully on the playground—but standing up to them and reporting their behavior will keep bullies in check. However, with cyber bullying there are several things you can do to help protect yourself from becoming a target. You can make it more difficult for bullies to use your digital life against you.

If bullying isn't stopped, it can become a chronic cycle that can last for years. It is a myth that bullying will go away when it is ignored.

Are You at Risk?

The behaviors listed below can put you at risk of cyber bullying. Answer "yes" or "no" to the following online acts. Each "yes" makes it more likely that you already have been, or soon will be, the victim of cyber bullying.

- Someone else knows my password for my email or for a social media website (other than my parents).

- I use chat rooms to talk to people I don't know in real life.

- I have a website with personal information about me and photos of me on it.

- I belong to a social networking website like Facebook, Formspring, or Twitter.

  - I have a blog that allows people to leave comments.

  - A person who knows me well might be able to guess my password.

  - I use a password hint to remember my passwords.

  - I have shared my photo with someone I met online.

  - I have shared secrets with friends online.

  - I have emailed embarrassing or nude photos of myself to someone else.

  - I have a guestbook on my website.

  - I have my cell number listed on a public website.

  - I accept instant messages from strangers.

How many times did you answer "yes"? If you answered "yes" even once, you should make an extra effort to protect yourself.

Amanda Todd

The case of Amanda Todd shows us how horrible and complex cyber bullying can be, especially when it is combined with physical, verbal, and social bullying.

Amanda's story began when she was in the seventh grade. While Web chatting, she met a man who told her she was beautiful and he convinced her to take off her top. This mistake took over her life. The unknown man captured an image of Amanda topless and used it to harass her—he sent the image to her friends and the next year he created a fake Facebook account in Amanda's name with the image as the profile picture.

It Didn't Stop

Instead of Amanda being able to rely on her friends for support during this crisis, she was rejected by the other kids at her school. When her photo was sent to all her classmates, she was humiliated and teased. She became anxious, depressed, and suffered from panic attacks. Amanda changed schools, but she again became the target of cyber, social, verbal, and physical abuse from her peers. She became involved with a boy who didn't tell her that he had a girlfriend. Later that girlfriend and some other girls beat Amanda up, and Amanda realized that the boy had been lying to her about his feelings.

When the rejection and abuse became too much, Amanda attempted suicide by drinking bleach. Again her peers bullied her online about her suicide attempt. She eventually moved to a different city, but the abuse continued. She turned to drugs, alcohol, and cutting herself to cope.

Telling Her Story

In September 2012, Amanda posted a video on YouTube telling her story. Complete strangers started to abuse her online, calling her stupid and slutty, and suggesting she deserved to die! Even though thousands of people around the world offered her support, the bullying was still too much for her to bear.

A few weeks later, Amanda took her own life.

It's easy for people to post nasty pictures, videos, and text from the safety of their computers. It doesn't feel real when it's on-screen. But it was real to Amanda, as it is to many other victims of cyber bullies. Those peers who abused her physically, verbally, and socially at school, and those who attacked her online, will have to live with the guilt of what they did for the rest of their lives.

Amanda's story may seem extreme, but it shows us how quickly a "little" thing can spiral out of control and how much the way we treat our peers can affect them. Let's hope that Amanda's tragic story will help save other young people from being bullied.

Are You a Cyber Bully?

Have you ever...

1. Signed on to email or a social networking site using another person's name and password?

2. Sent an email or online greeting card from someone else's account?

3. Forwarded a private IM or email without the writer's permission?

4. Hacked into someone's account or their password-protected computer?

5. Posted rude, nasty, or hurtful comments about someone online?

6. Teased or frightened someone during IM chats?

7. Joined an online clique or chat room that singled out others or made them unwelcome?

8. Accused someone of doing something online without any proof?

9. Followed someone all over the Web, from blog to chat room to social media site?

If you answered "yes" to any of the above questions, you may be a cyber bully. Some of these actions may not seem all that bad, such as forwarding a private message without permission. Maybe you only did it once? Or maybe you didn't intend to hurt anyone? But remember, on the Internet, nothing can be undone. Once you send that private message, it's not private anymore.

Tips for Protecting Yourself Against Cyber Bullying

- Never give out personal contact information about yourself, your parents, or your friends—such as your name, address, phone number, age, or email address.

- Never share intimate personal information or personal interests, such as your city or school name.

- Never give out passwords to anyone other than your parents, not even your best friend.

- Never send or post embarrassing pictures of yourself to your friends or a website, even if you think it is private.

- Never write anything in an email or text message or a blog post that you wouldn't feel comfortable telling your parents or your entire class!

- Treat all of your online friends the way you want to be treated. Be respectful of others, and avoid gossiping and making fun of others online.

Think About It!

What will you do the next time you get an embarrassing or mean text message, email, or photo about one of your classmates? Have you liked a Facebook page that posts nasty things about people? If yes, why have you? What do you think about retweeting gossip or hurtful tweets? Have you watched a friend send mean or threatening messages and not tried to stop them or report their behavior?

Other Resources

If you are dealing with bullying—either as a target, bystander, or bully—you don't have to go through it alone. There is information out there and people who are waiting to help. Don't hesitate to reach out if you need them.

Books

Cyberbullying Prevention and Response: Expert Perspectives by Justin W. Patchin and Sameer Hinduja (Routledge, 2012)

This book, by professors of criminal justice, explores the major issues that teachers, school administrators, counselors, social workers, and parents need to be aware of when it comes to identifying, preventing, and responding to cyber bullying.

Teen Cyberbullying Investigated: Where do Your Rights End and Consequences Begin? by Tom Jacobs (Free Spirit Publishing, 2010)

In this book, Judge Tom Jacobs reviews court cases involving teens charged with cyber bullying in the United States. The cases include many different kinds of cyber bullying, and the book explores the decisions and asks readers to think about how such behavior can affect their lives.

Websites

End to Cyber Bullying (ETCB) Organization
www.endcyberbullying.org

The ETCB was founded in 2011 with the goal of creating a social network free of bullying. This organization is seeking to educate people about what they can do to prevent cyber bullying. The website is a great source for more information.

PACER Center's Teens Against Bullying
www.pacerteensagainstbullying.org

Teens Against Bullying is an organization started by kids for kids. On the website, young people can talk about their experiences, learn more about bullying, and how to prevent it.

Cyberbullying Research Center
www.cyberbullying.us

Dr. Justin W. Patchin and Dr. Sameer Hinduja launched this website in 2005 to create a resource for parents, teachers, counselors, and law enforcement. The site provides access to sound research in the area of cyber bullying, which Dr. Patchin and Dr. Hinduja have been studying since 2002. These researchers have developed resources for teens about using electronic communication.

Facebook Family Safety Center
https://www.facebook.com/safety/

On this page, Facebook provides information, tools, and resources for parents and teens about how to use Facebook safely and responsibly.

Organizations, Hotlines, and Helplines

Kids Help Phone (Canada) (1-800-668-6868)
www.kidshelpphone.ca

Kids Help Phone provides youth across Canada with 24/7 access to counselors, both online and on the phone. You can talk to Kids Help Phone about anything at anytime and get help. It's anonymous, confidential, and nonjudgmental. The counselors can also help you find some help in your local community.

Boys Town National Hotline (United States) (1-800-448-3000)
www.yourlifeyourvoice.org

In the United States, you can call this national hotline to talk to a counselor about anything at anytime. This hotline can help you find help in your local community or just talk to you about how you're feeling.

My Gay Straight Alliance (Canada) (www.mygsa.ca)
MGSA.ca is Canada's website for safer and inclusive schools for the lesbian, gay, bisexual, trans, queer, and questioning (LGBTQ) community.

The Trevor Project (United States) (866-4-U-TREVOR)
www.thetrevorproject.org

The Trevor Project provides crisis intervention and suicide prevention services to lesbian, gay, bisexual, transgender, and questioning youth.

Glossary

anonymous Not named or identified

bullying Repeated, aggressive behavior intended to hurt and to gain power over the victim

bystander A person who is present at an event but does not take part

bystander effect An event where the greater the number of people present, the less likely people are to help a person in distress

cyber bullying Using technology (email, texts, blogs, social networking sites) to intimidate a person, hurt their feelings or damage their reputation

direct bullying Bullying that happens directly to the target, such as punching or insults

empathy The act of understanding and identifying with the feelings of others

ethical behavior Behavior that involves decisions about what is right and wrong

forum A place that provides an opportunity for discussion, either in person, in the media, or online

harassment The act of annoying or attacking a person often

hate crime A crime that is motivated by hatred or intolerance of a specific group of people based on race, gender, sexual orientation, religion, or other category

hate speech Speech or writing that expresses hate or intolerance of a specific group of people based on race, gender, sexual orientation, religion, or other category

indirect bullying Bullying that happens behind the target's back, such as starting hurtful rumors

instant messaging (IM) An instant text message sent over the Internet

malicious gossip Gossip that is intended to harm a person

pornography Pictures or writings describing sexual behavior and intended to cause sexual excitement

social bullying Intentionally damaging someone's social life/relationships by excluding someone from a group on purpose, spreading rumors, or telling others to avoid that person (also known as relational bullying)

social media Online communities in which users share information, ideas, personal messages, and other content

target The person selected as the aim of an attack

traditional bullying Bullying that doesn't involve digital communication

traumatic Relating to severe emotional distress

witness A person who sees something happen

Index